GOVERNMENT IN THE FUTURE

GOVERNMENT IN THE FUTURE

Noam Chomsky

Open Media Pamphlet Series

SEVEN STORIES PRESS
New York

Open Media Series Editor: Greg Ruggiero

Seven Stories Press
140 Watts Street
New York, NY 10013
www.sevenstories.com

In Canada:
Publishers Group Canada, 250A Carlton Street, Toronto, ON M5A-2L1

In the UK:
Turnaround Publisher Services Ltd., Unit 3, Olympia Trading Estate, Coburg Road, Wood Green, London N22 6TZ

In Australia:
Palgrave Macmillan, 627 Chapel Street, South Yarra VIC 3141

ISBN-10: 1-58322-685-0 / ISBN-13: 978-1-58322-685-8

Book design by Jon Gilbert

9 8 7 6 5 4 3 2

College professors may order examination copies of Seven Stories Press titles for a free six-month trial period. To order, visit www.sevenstories.com/text-book, or fax on school letterhead to (212) 226-1411.

Printed in Canada.

GOVERNMENT IN THE FUTURE

Based on a talk given at the Poetry Center,
New York City, February 16, 1970

What is the role of the state in an advanced industrial society? To answer that question, I think it's useful to set up as a framework for discussion four somewhat idealized positions. I want to call these positions, first, *classical liberal,* second, *libertarian socialist,* third, *state socialist,* fourth, *state capitalist.* And I want to consider each in turn. Also, I want to make clear my own point of view in advance, so that you can better evaluate and judge what I am saying. I think that the libertarian socialist concepts—and by that I mean a range of thinking that extends from left-wing Marxism through anarchism—are fundamentally correct and that they are the proper and natural extensions of classical liberalism into the current era of advanced industrial society.

In contrast, it seems to me that the ideology of state socialism, that is, what has become of Bolshevism and of state capitalism—the modern welfare state—are regressive and highly inadequate social theories, and a large number of our really fundamental problems stem from a kind of incompatibility and inappropriateness of these dominant social forms to modern industrial societies.

Well, then, let me consider these four points of reference in sequence—beginning with the classical liberal point of view.

Classical Liberalism

Classical liberalism asserts as its major idea an opposition to all but the most restricted and minimal forms of state intervention in personal and social life. This conclusion is quite familiar. However, the reasoning that leads to it is less familiar and I think a good deal more important than the conclusion itself.

One of the earliest and most brilliant expositions of this position is in Wilhelm von Humboldt's *Limits of State Action*, which was written in 1792, though not published as a book until sixty years after that. In his view, the state tends to "make man an instrument to serve its arbitrary ends, overlooking his individual purposes,"[1] and since humans are in their essence free, searching, self-perfecting beings, it follows that the state is a profoundly antihuman institution. That is, its actions and existence are ultimately incompatible with the full harmonious development of human potential in its richest diversity—hence incompatible with what Humboldt and, in the following century, Marx, Bakunin, Mill, and many others saw as the true end of man. (And, for the record, I think that this is an accurate description.)

In this sense, the modern conservative tends to regard himself as the lineal descendant of the classical liberal. But I think that can only be maintained from an extremely superficial point of view, as one can see by studying more carefully the fundamental ideas of classical libertarian thought, expressed in my opinion in its most profound form by Humboldt.

I think the issues are of quite considerable contemporary significance, and if you don't mind what may appear to be a somewhat antiquarian excursion, I'd like to expand on them.

For Humboldt, as for Rousseau and before him the Cartesians, man's central attribute is his freedom.

To inquire and to create—these are the centres around which all human pursuits more or less directly revolve.[2]

But he goes on to say that

all moral culture springs solely and immediately from the inner life of the soul, and can . . . never [be] produced by external and artificial contrivances. . . . The cultivation of the understanding, as any of man's other faculties, is generally achieved by his own activity, his own ingenuity, or his own methods of using the discoveries of others.[3]

From these assumptions Humboldt develops an educational theory, though I won't pursue it now. But also far more follows. Humboldt goes on to develop the rudiments of a theory of exploitation and of alienated labor that suggests in significant ways, I think, the early Marx. Humboldt in fact continues the comments that I quoted about the cultivation of the understanding through spontaneous action in the following way. He says that "man never regards what he possesses as so much his own, as what he does; and the labourer who tends a garden is perhaps in a truer sense its owner, than the listless voluptuary who enjoys its fruits."[4] And since truly human action is that which flows from inner impulse,

> it seems as if all peasants and craftsmen might be elevated into artists; that is, men who love labour for its own sake, improve it by their own plastic genius and inventive skill, and thereby cultivate their intellect, ennoble their character, and exalt and refine their pleasures. And so humanity would be ennobled by the very things which now, though beautiful in themselves, so often serve to degrade it. . . . [F]reedom is undoubtedly the indispensable condition, without which even the pursuits most congenial to individual human nature, can never succeed in producing such salutary influences. Whatever does not spring from a man's free choice, or is

only the result of instruction and guidance, does not enter into his very being, but remains alien to his true nature; he does not perform it with truly human energies, but merely with mechanical exactness.[5]

And if a man acts in a mechanical way, reacting to external demands or instructions rather than in ways determined by his own interests and energies and power, "we may admire what he does, but we despise what he is."[6]

For Humboldt, then, man is born to inquire and create, and when a man or a child chooses to inquire or create out of his own free choice, then he becomes in his own terms an artist rather than a tool of production or a well-trained parrot. This is the essence of his concept of human nature. And I think that it is very revealing and interesting compared with Marx, with the early Marx manuscripts, and particularly his account of "the alienation of labor when work is external to the worker, . . . not part of his nature, . . . [so that] he does not fulfill himself in his work but denies himself . . . [and is] physically exhausted and mentally debased," alienated labor that "casts some of the workers back into a barbarous kind of work and turns others into machines," thus depriving man of his "species character," of "free conscious activity," and "productive life."[7]

Recall also Marx's well-known and often-quoted reference to a higher form of society in which "labour has become not only a means of life but life's prime want."[8] And recall also his repeated criticism of the specialized labor processes that "mutilate the labourer into a fragment of a man, degrade him to the level of an appendage of a machine, destroy every remnant of charm in his work and turn it into a hated toil; . . . [and] estrange from him the intellectual potentialities of the labour-process in the same proportion as science is incorporated into it as an independent power."[9]

14

Robert Tucker, for one, has rightly emphasized that Marx sees the revolutionary more as the frustrated producer than as a dissatisfied consumer. And this far more radical critique of capitalist relations of production flows directly, often in the same words, from the libertarian thought of the Enlightenment. For this reason, I think, one must say that classical liberal ideas in their essence, though not in the way they developed, are profoundly anticapitalist. The essence of these ideas must be destroyed for them to serve as an ideology of modern industrial capitalism.

Writing in the 1780s and early 1790s, Humboldt had no conception of the forms that industrial capitalism would take. Consequently, in this classic of classical liberalism he stresses the problem of limiting *state* power, and he is not overly concerned with the dangers of *private* power. The reason is that he believes in, and speaks of, the essential equality of conditions of private citizens. And of course he had no idea, writing in 1790, of the ways in which the notion of a private person would come to be reinterpreted in the era of corporate capitalism. He did not foresee—I now quote the anarchist historian Rudolf Rocker—that "Democracy with its motto of 'equality of all citizens before the law,' and Liberalism with its 'right of man over his own person,' both [would be] shipwrecked on the realities of the capitalist economic form."[10] Humboldt did not foresee that in a predatory capitalistic economy, state intervention would be an absolute necessity to preserve human existence and prevent the destruction of the physical environment. I speak optimistically, of course. As Karl Polanyi, for one, has pointed out, the self-adjusting market "could not exist for any length of time without annihilating the human and natural substance of society; it would have physically destroyed man and transformed his surroundings into a wilderness."[11] I think that is correct. Humboldt also did not foresee the consequences of the commodity character of labor, the doctrine, again in Polanyi's words, that "it is not for the commodity to decide where it should be offered for sale, to what purpose it should be used, at what price it should be allowed to change hands, and in what manner it should be consumed or destroyed."[12] But the commodity is, of course, in this case, human life, and social protection was therefore a minimal necessity to constrain the irrational and destructive workings of the classical free market. Nor did Humboldt understand in 1790 that capitalist economic relations perpetuated a form of bondage that, as early as 1767, Simon Linguet had declared to be even worse than slavery.

> It is the impossibility of living by any other means that compels our farm labourers to till the soil whose fruits they will not eat, and our masons to construct buildings in which they will not live. It is want that drags them to those

markets where they await masters who will do them the kindness of buying them. *It is want that compels them to go down on their knees to the rich man in order to get from him permission to enrich him. . . .* [W]hat effective gain the *suppression of slavery* has brought to them. I say with as much sorrow as frankness: all that they have gained is to be every moment tormented by the fear of death from hunger, a calamity that at least never visited their predecessors in this lowest rank of mankind. . . . "He is free, you say. Ah! That is his misfortune.["] . . . These men, it is said, have no master . . . they have one, and the most terrible, the most imperious of masters, that is, *need*. It is this that reduces them to the most cruel dependence.[13]

And if there is something degrading to human nature in the idea of bondage, as every spokesman for the Enlightenment would insist, then it would follow that a new emancipation must be awaited, what Fourier referred to as the "third and last emancipatory phase of history"—the first having made serfs out of slaves, the second wage earners out of serfs—which will transform the proletariat into free men by eliminating the commodity character of labor, ending wage slavery, and bringing the commercial, industrial, and financial institutions under democratic control.[14]

These are all things that Humboldt in his classical liberal doctrine did not express and didn't see, but I think that he might have accepted these conclusions. He does, for example, agree that state intervention in social life is legitimate "if freedom would destroy the very conditions without which not only freedom but even existence itself would be inconceivable," which are precisely the circumstances that arise in an unconstrained capitalist economy.[15] And he does, as in the remarks that I quoted, vigorously condemn the alienation of labor.

In any event, his criticism of bureaucracy and the autocratic state stands as a very eloquent forewarning of some of the most dismal aspects of modern history. And the important point is that the basis of his critique is applicable to a far broader range of coercive institutions than he imagined—in particular to the institutions of industrial capitalism.

Though he expresses a classical liberal doctrine, Humboldt is no primitive individualist, in the style of, for example, Rousseau. Rousseau extols the savage who "lives within himself,"[16] but Humboldt's vision is entirely different. He sums up his remarks, saying that

> the whole tenor of the ideas and arguments unfolded in this essay might fairly be reduced to this, that while they would break all fetters in human society, they would attempt to find as many new social bonds as possible. The isolated man is no more able to develop than the one who is fettered.[17]

And he in fact looks forward to a community of free association without coercion by the state or other authoritarian institutions, in which free men can create, inquire, and achieve the highest development of their powers. In fact, far ahead of his time, he presents an anarchist vision that is appropriate perhaps to the next stage of industrial society. We can perhaps look forward to a day when these various strands will be brought together within the framework of libertarian socialism, a social form that barely exists today, though its elements can perhaps be perceived, for example, in the guarantee of individual rights that has achieved so far its fullest realization—though still tragically flawed—in the Western democracies; in the Israeli kibbutzim; in the experiments of workers' councils in Yugoslavia; in the effort to awaken popular consciousness and create a new involvement in the social process, which is a fundamental element in the Third World revolutions that coexists uneasily with indefensible authoritarian practices.

To summarize, the first concept of the state that I want to establish as a point of reference is classical liberalism. Its doctrine is that state functions should be drastically limited. But this familiar characterization is a very superficial one. More deeply, the classical liberal view develops from a certain concept of human nature, one that stresses the importance of diversity and free creation, and therefore this view is in fundamental opposition to industrial capitalism with its wage slavery, its alienated labor, and its hierarchic and authoritarian principles of social and economic organization. At least in its ideal form, classical liberal thought is opposed to the concepts of possessive individualism, that are intrinsic to capitalist ideology. For this reason, classical liberal thought seeks to eliminate social fetters and to replace them with social bonds, and not with competitive greed, predatory individualism, and not, of course, with corporate empires—state or private. Classical libertarian thought seems to me, therefore, to lead directly to libertarian socialism, or anarchism if you like, when combined with an understanding of industrial capitalism.

Libertarian Socialism

The second point of reference that I want to discuss is the libertarian socialist vision of the state. A French writer rather sympathetic to anarchism once wrote that "anarchism has a broad back, like paper, it endures anything."[18] And there are many shades of anarchism. But I am concerned here only with one, namely the anarchism of Bakunin, who wrote in his anarchist manifesto of 1865 that to be an anarchist one must first be a socialist. I am also concerned with the anarchism of Adolph Fischer, one of the martyrs of the Haymarket affair in 1886, who said that "every anarchist is a socialist, but every socialist is not necessarily an anarchist."[19] A consistent anarchist must oppose private ownership of the means of production. Such property is indeed, as Proudhon in his famous remark asserted, a form of theft.[20] But a consistent anarchist will also oppose "the organisation of production by Government. It means State-socialism, the command of the State-officials over production and the command of managers, scientists, shop-officials in the shop. . . . The goal of the working class is liberation from exploitation. This goal is not reached and cannot be reached by a new directing and governing class substituting [itself for] the bourgeoisie. It is only realised by the workers themselves being master over production,"[21] by some form of workers' councils. These remarks, it happens, are quoted from the left-wing Marxist Anton Pannekoek. It is an important point, I think, that radical Marxism—what Lenin once called infantile

ultraleftism[22]—merges with anarchist currents.
Let me give one further illustration of this con-
vergence between left-wing Marxism and
socialist anarchism. Consider the following
characterization of "revolutionary socialism":

> The revolutionary Socialist denies that State
> ownership can end in anything other than a
> bureaucratic despotism. We have seen why the
> State cannot democratically control industry.
> Industry can only be democratically owned
> and controlled by the workers electing directly
> from their own ranks industrial administrative
> committees. Socialism will be fundamentally
> an industrial system; its constituencies will be
> of an industrial character. Thus those carrying
> on the social activities and industries of society
> will be directly represented in the local and cen-
> tral industrial councils of social administration.
> In this way the powers of such delegates will
> flow upwards from those carrying on the work
> and conversant with the needs of the commu-
> nity. When the central administrative indus-
> trial committee meets it will represent every

phase of social activity. Hence the capitalist political or geographical state will be replaced by the industrial administrative committee of Socialism. The transition from the one social system to the other will be the *social revolution.* The political State throughout history has meant the government *of men* by ruling classes; the Republic of Socialism will be the government *of industry* administered on behalf of the whole community. The former meant the economic and political subjection of the many; the latter will mean the economic freedom of all—it will be, therefore, a true democracy.[23]

These remarks are taken from a book called *The State: Its Origins and Function,* written by William Paul in early 1917, just prior to Lenin's *State and Revolution,* which is his most libertarian work.

William Paul was one of the founders of the British Communist Party, later the editor of the British Communist Party journal. It is interesting that his critique of state socialism resembles—very closely, I think—the libertarian doctrine of the anarchists, particularly in its principle that the state must disappear, to be replaced by the industrial organization of society in the course of the social revolution itself. Proudhon in 1851 wrote that what we put in place of the government is industrial organization, and many similar comments can be cited. That, in essence, is the fundamental idea of anarchist revolutionaries.

What's more important than the fact that many such statements can be cited is that these ideas have been realized in spontaneous revolutionary action several times, for example, in Germany and Italy after World War I, and in Catalonia in 1936.

One might argue, at least I would argue, that council communism—in the sense of the long quotation that I read—is the natural form of revolutionary socialism in an industrial society. It reflects the intuitive understanding that democracy is largely a sham when the industrial system is controlled by any form of autocratic elite, whether it's owners, managers, technocrats, a vanguard party, a state bureaucracy, or whatever. Under conditions of authoritarian domination, the classical liberal ideals, which are expressed also by Marx and Bakunin and all true revolutionaries, cannot be realized. Human beings will not, in other words, be free to inquire and create, to develop their own potentialities to their fullest; the worker will remain a fragment of a human, degraded, a tool in the productive process directed from above. In this sense, the ideas of revolutionary libertarian socialism have been submerged in the industrial societies of the past half century. The dominant ideologies have been those of state socialism and state capitalism.

But there has been an interesting resurgence in the last couple of years. The theses I quoted by Anton Pannekoek were taken from a recent pamphlet of a radical French workers' group,[24] and the remarks by William Paul on revolutionary socialism are cited in a paper by Walter Kendall given at the National Conference on Workers' Control in Sheffield, England, in March 1969.[25]

Both of these groups represent something significant. In particular, the workers' control movement in England has developed, I think, into a remarkably significant force in the last few years. It includes some of the largest trade unions, for example, including the Amalgamated Engineering and Foundryworkers' Union, which I think is the second-largest trade union in England, and which has taken these principles as its fundamental ideas. It's had a series of successful conferences that have put out an interesting pamphlet literature. And on the continent there are parallel developments. May 1968 in France accelerated the growing interest in council communism and similar ideas, as well as other forms of libertarian socialism, in France, Germany, and England. Given the general conservative cast of our highly ideological society, it's not too surprising that the United States has been relatively untouched by these currents. But that, too, may change. The erosion of the Cold War mythology at least makes it possible to discuss some of these questions. And if the present wave of repression can be beaten back, if the left can overcome its more suicidal tendencies and build on the achievements of the past decade, the problem of how to organize industrial society on truly democratic lines, with democratic control in the workplace as well as in the community, should become the dominant intellectual issue for those who are alive to the problems of contemporary society. And as a mass movement for revolutionary libertarian socialism develops, as I hope it will, speculation should proceed to action.

Now, it may seem quixotic to group left Marxism and anarchism under the same rubric

as I have done, given the antagonism throughout the past century between Marxists and anarchists—beginning with the antagonism
between Marx and Engels on the one hand and,
for example, Proudhon and Bakunin on the
other. In the nineteenth century, their differ-
ences with regard to the question of the state
were significant, but in a sense they were tacti-
cal. The anarchists were convinced that capitalism and the state must be destroyed together.
Engels, in a letter of 1883, expressed his opposition to the idea as follows:

> The anarchists put the thing upside down.
> They declare that the proletarian revolution
> must *begin* by doing away with the political
> organisation of the state. . . . But to destroy it
> at such a moment would be to destroy the only
> organism by means of which the victorious
> proletariat can assert its newly-conquered
> power, hold down its capitalist adversaries and
> carry out that economic revolution of society
> without which the whole victory must end in

a new defeat and in a mass slaughter of the workers similar to those after the Paris Commune.[26]

Now, the Paris commune, I think it is fair to say, did represent ideas of libertarian socialism, of anarchism, if you like, and Marx, of course, wrote about it with great enthusiasm. His experience of the commune, in fact, led him to modify his concept of the role of the state and to take on something of a more anarchist perspective with regard to the nature of social revolution, as you can see, for example, by looking at the introduction to the 1872 edition of *The Communist Manifesto.*[27]

Well, the commune was, of course, drowned in blood, as the anarchist communes of Spain were destroyed by the Fascist and the Communist armies. And it might be argued that more dictatorial structures would have defended the revolution against such forces. But I doubt this very much. At least in the case of Spain, it seems to me that a more consistent libertarian policy might have provided the only possible defense of the revolution. Of course, this can be contested and this is a long story that I don't want to go into here, but at the very least it's clear that one would have to be rather naive after the events of the past half century to fail to see the truth in Bakunin's repeated warnings that the "red bureaucracy" would prove to be "the vilest and most dangerous lie of our century."[28] He once said in 1870, "Take the most radical of revolutionaries and place him on the throne of all the Russias or give him dictatorial powers . . . and before the year is out he will be worse than the Czar himself."[29]

In this respect Bakunin was all too perceptive, and this kind of warning was repeatedly voiced from the left. For example, in the 1890s the anarchosyndicalist Fernand Pelloutier asked, "But must the transitional state to be endured necessarily or inevitably be the collectivist jail? Might it not consist of libertarian organization confined to the needs of production and consumption alone, with all political institutions having been done away with?"[30]

I don't pretend to know the answer to that question, but I think that it is tolerably clear that unless the answer is positive, the chances for a truly democratic revolution that will achieve the humanistic ideals of the left are perhaps rather slight. I think Martin Buber put the problem quite succinctly when he said: "One cannot in the nature of things expect a little tree that has been turned into a club to put forth leaves."[31] For just this reason, it's essential that a powerful revolutionary movement exist in the United States if there are to be any reasonable possibilities for democratic social change of a radical sort anywhere in the capitalist world. And comparable remarks I think undoubtedly hold for the Russian empire.

Until the end of his life, Lenin stressed the idea that it is an "elementary truth of Marxism, that the victory of socialism requires the joint efforts of workers in a number of advanced countries."[32] At the very least it requires that domestic pressures impede the great centers of world imperialism from counterrevolutionary intervention. Only such possibilities will permit any revolution to overthrow its own coercive state institutions as it tries to bring the economy under direct democratic control.

Let me summarize briefly again. I have mentioned so far two reference points for discussion of the state: classical liberalism and libertarian socialism. Ideologically, they are in agreement that the functions of the state are repressive and that state action must be limited. The libertarian socialist goes on to insist that state power must be eliminated in favor of democratic organization of industrial society, with direct popular control over all institutions by those

35

who participate in—as well as those who are directly affected by—the workings of these institutions. So one might imagine a system of workers' councils, consumers' councils, commune assemblies, regional federations, and so on, with the kind of representation that's direct and revocable, in the sense that representatives are directly answerable to and return directly to the well-defined and integrated social group for which they speak in some higher order organization—something obviously very different than our system of representation.

Counterarguments

It might very well be asked whether such a social structure is feasible in a complex, highly technological society. There are counterarguments, and I think they fall into two main categories. The first category is that such an organization is contrary to human nature, and the second category says roughly that it is incompatible with the demands of efficiency. I'd like to briefly consider each of these.

Consider the first counterargument—that a free society is contrary to human nature. It is often asked, if people really want freedom, do they want the responsibility that goes with it, or would they prefer to be ruled by a benevolent master? Consistently, apologists for the existing distribution of power have held to one or another version of the idea of the happy slave. Two hundred years ago, Rousseau denounced the sophistic politicians and intellectuals who searched for ways to obscure the fact, so he maintained, that the essential and defining property of human beings is their freedom: "[T]hey attribute to men a natural inclination to servitude, . . . without thinking that it is the same for freedom as for innocence and virtue—their value is felt only as long as

37

one enjoys them oneself and the taste for them is lost as soon as one has lost them."[33] As proof of this doctrine, he refers to the marvels done by all free peoples to guard themselves from oppression. True, he says, those who have abandoned the life of the free,

> do nothing but boast incessantly of the peace and repose they enjoy in their chains. . . . But when I see the others sacrifice pleasures, repose, wealth, power and life itself for the preservation of this sole good which is so disdained by those who have lost it; . . . when I see multitudes of entirely naked savages scorn European voluptuousness and endure hunger, fire, the sword, and death to preserve only their independence, I feel it does not behoove slaves to reason about freedom.[34]

A comment to which we can perhaps give a contemporary interpretation.

Rather similar thoughts were expressed by Kant forty years later. He could not, he said, accept the proposition that certain people are "not yet ripe for freedom," for example, the serfs of some landlord.

> If one accepts this assumption, freedom will never be achieved; for one cannot arrive at the maturity for freedom without having already acquired it; one must be free to learn how to make use of one's powers freely and usefully. The first attempts will surely be brutal and will lead to a state of affairs more painful and dangerous than the former condition, under the dominance but also the protection of an external authority. However, one can achieve reason only through one's own experiences, and one must be free to undertake them. . . . To accept the principle that freedom is worthless for those under one's control and that one has the right to refuse it to them forever, is an infringement on the right of God himself, who has created man to be free.[35]

This particular remark is interesting because of its context as well. Kant was defending the

French Revolution during the terror against those who claimed it showed the masses to be unready for the privilege of freedom. And I think that his remarks, too, have contemporary relevance. No rational person will approve of violence and terror, in particular the terror of the postrevolutionary states that have fallen into the hands of a grim autocracy, and have more than once reached indescribable levels of savagery. At the same time, no person of understanding or humanity will too quickly condemn the violence that often occurs when long-subdued masses rise against their oppressors or take their first steps toward liberty and social reconstruction.

Humboldt, just a few years before Kant, had expressed a view that was very similar to that. He also said that freedom and variety are the preconditions for human self-realization:

> [N]othing promotes this ripeness for freedom so much as freedom itself. This truth, perhaps,

may not be acknowledged by those who have so often used this unripeness as an excuse for continuing repression. But it seems to me to follow unquestionably from the very nature of man. The incapacity for freedom can only arise from a want of moral and intellectual power; to heighten this power is the only way to supply the want; but to do this presupposes the exercise of the power, and this exercise presupposes the freedom which awakens spontaneous activity.[36]

Those who do not comprehend this, he says, "may justly be suspected of misunderstanding human nature, and of wishing to make men into machines."[37]

Rosa Luxemburg's fraternal and sympathetic critique of Bolshevik ideology and practice was given in very similar terms. Only the active participation of the masses in self-government and social reconstruction could bring about what she described as the complete spiritual transformation in the masses degraded by centuries of bourgeois class rule, just as only their creative experience and spontaneous action could solve the myriad problems of creating a libertarian socialist society. She went on to say that "Historically, the errors committed by a truly revolutionary movement are infinitely more fruitful than the infallibility of the cleverest Central Committee."[38] And I think that these remarks can be translated immediately for the somewhat parallel ideology of the "soulful corporation," which is now fairly popular among American academics, for example, Carl Kaysen, who writes:

> No longer the agent of proprietorships seeking to maximize return on investment, management sees itself as responsible to stockholders, employees, customers, the general public, and perhaps most important the firm itself as an institution. . . . [T]here is no display of greed and graspingness; there is no attempt to push off onto the workers or the community at large

part of the social costs of the enterprise. The modern corporation is a soulful corporation.[39]

Similarly, the vanguard party is a soulful party, and in both cases those who urge that men submit to the rule of these benevolent autocracies may, I think, justly be accused of "wishing to make men into machines."

Now, I don't think that the correctness of the view, which is expressed by Rousseau and Kant and Humboldt and Luxemburg and innumerable others, is for the moment susceptible to scientific proof. One can only evaluate it in terms of experience and intuition. One can also point out the social consequences of adopting the view that men are born to be free, or that they are born to be ruled by benevolent autocrats.

What of the second counterargument, the question of efficiency? Is democratic control of the industrial system down to its smallest functional unit incompatible with efficiency? This is very frequently argued on several grounds. Some say, for example, that centralized management is a technological imperative, but I think the argument is exceedingly weak when one looks into it. The very same technology that brings relevant information to the board of managers can bring it at the time that it is needed to everyone in the workforce. The technology that's now capable of eliminating the stupefying labor that turns people into specialized tools of production permits, in principle, the leisure and the educational opportunities that make them able to use this information in a rational way. And furthermore, even an economic elite that is "dripping with soulfulness"—to use Ralph Miliband's phrase—is constrained by the system in which it functions to organize production for certain ends: power, growth, profit, but not—in the nature of the case—human needs, needs that to an ever more critical degree can be expressed only in collective terms.[40] It is surely conceiv-

44

able and is perhaps even likely that decisions made by the collective itself will reflect these needs and interests as well as those made by various soulful elites.

In any event, it is a bit difficult to take seriously arguments about efficiency in a society that devotes enormous resources to waste and destruction. As everyone knows, the very concept of efficiency is dripping with ideology. Maximization of commodities is hardly the only measure of a decent existence.

State Socialism and State Capitalism

Well, let me turn finally to the third and fourth points of reference, Bolshevism—or state socialism—and state capitalism. As I have tried to suggest, they have points in common, and in interesting respects they diverge from the classical liberal ideal, and its later elaboration in libertarian socialism. Since I am concerned with our society, let me make a few rather elementary observations about the role of the state, its likely evolution, and the ideological assumptions that accompany and sometimes disguise these phenomena. To begin with, we can distinguish two systems of power, the political system and the economic system. The former consists in principle of elected representatives of the people who set public policy; the latter, in principle, is a system of private power—a system of private empires—that are free from public control, except in the remote and indirect ways in which even a feudal nobility or a totalitarian dictatorship must be responsive to the public will. There are several immediate consequences of this organization of society. The first is that in a subtle way, an authoritarian cast of mind is induced in a very large mass of the population, which is subject to arbitrary decree from above. And I think that this has a great effect on the general character of the culture: the belief that one must obey arbitrary dictates and accede to authority. And I think that a remarkable and exciting fact about the youth movement in recent years is that it's challenging and beginning to break down some of these authoritarian patterns.

An important second fact is that the range of decisions that are in principle subject to public democratic control is quite narrow. For example, it excludes in law and in principle the central institutions in any advanced industrial society, that is, the entire commercial, industrial, and financial system.

And a third fact is that even within the narrow range of issues that are submitted in principle to democratic decision making, the centers of private power exert an inordinately heavy influence in perfectly obvious ways, through control of the media, through control of political organizations, or by the simple and direct means of supplying the top personnel for the parliamentary system itself, as they obviously do. In Richard Barnet's recent study of the top four hundred decision makers in the postwar national security system, he finds that most "have come from executive suites and law offices within shouting distance of one another in fifteen city blocks in New York, Washington, Detroit, Chicago, and Boston."[41] And every other study shows the same thing.

In short, the democratic system at best functions within a narrow range in a capitalist democracy, and even within this narrow range its functioning is enormously biased by the concentrations of private power and by the authoritarian and passive modes of thinking that are induced by autocratic institutions such as industries. It's a truism, but one that must be constantly stressed, that capitalism and democracy are ultimately quite incompatible. A careful look at the matter, I think, merely strengthens this conclusion. There are processes of centralization of control taking place in both the political and the industrial system. As far as the political system is concerned, in every parliamentary democracy, not only ours, the role of parliament in policy formation has been declining since World War II. The executive, in other words, becomes increasingly powerful as the planning functions of the state become more significant. The House Armed Services Committee a couple of years ago described the role of Congress as that of a "sometimes querulous but essentially kindly uncle who complains while furiously puffing on his pipe but who finally, as everyone expects, gives in . . . and hands over the allowance."[42]

And careful studies of civil-military decisions since World War II show that this is quite an accurate perception. Senator Vandenberg twenty years ago expressed his fear that the American chief executive would become "the number one warlord of the earth."[43] That has since occurred.

The clearest expression of this is the decision to escalate in Vietnam in February 1965 in cynical disregard of the expressed will of the electorate. This incident reveals with perfect clarity the role of the public in decisions about peace and war, and the role of the public in decisions about the main lines of public policy in general; it also suggests the irrelevance of electoral politics to major decisions of national policy.

Unfortunately, you can't vote the rascals *out*, because you never voted them *in* in the first place. The corporate executives and corporation lawyers and so on who overwhelmingly staff the executive (assisted increasingly by a university-based managerial class) remain in power no matter whom you elect. And furthermore, it is interesting to note that this ruling elite is pretty clear about its social role. As an example, take Robert McNamara, the person who is widely praised in liberal circles for his humanity, his technical brilliance, and his campaign to control the military. His views of social organization, I think, are quite illuminating. He says "vital decision-making . . . particularly in policy matters, must remain at the top." And he goes on to suggest that this is apparently a divine imperative:

> God . . . is clearly democratic. He distributes brainpower universally, but He quite justifiably expects us to do something efficient and constructive with that priceless gift. That is what management is all about. . . . Management is in the end the most creative of all the arts for its medium is human talent itself. The real threat to democracy comes . . . from undermanagement. . . . To undermanage reality is not to keep it free. It is simply to let some force other than reason shape reality. . . . If it is not reason that rules man, then man falls short of his potential.[44]

So reason, then, is to be identified as the centralization of decision making at the top in the hands of management. Popular involvement in decision making is a threat to liberty, a violation of reason. Reason is embodied in autocratic, tightly managed institutions.

Strengthening these institutions within which man can function most efficiently, is, in his words, "the great human adventure of our times."[45]

All this has a faintly familiar ring to it, and I think it is the authentic voice of the technical intelligentsia, the liberal intelligentsia, of the technocratic corporate elite in a modern society. There is a parallel process of centralization in economic life. A recent Federal Trade Commission (FTC) report notes that "[b]y the end of 1968, the two hundred largest industrial corporations controlled over 60 percent of the total assets held by all manufacturing corporations." At the beginning of World War II the same amount of power was spread over a thousand corporations. The report observes that a small industrial elite of huge conglomerate companies is gobbling up American business and largely destroying competitive free enterprise.[46]

Furthermore, these two hundred corporations are partially linked with each other and with other corporations in ways that may prevent or discourage independent behavior in market decisions.

What is novel about such observations is only their source: the FTC. They are familiar to the point of cliché among left-liberal commentators on American society.

The centralization of power also has an international dimension. It's been pointed out that—I am quoting from *Foreign Affairs*—"on the basis of the gross value of their output, U.S. enterprises abroad in the aggregate comprise the third largest economy . . . in the world—with a gross product greater than that of any country except the United States and the Soviet Union."[47]

Within a decade, given present trends, more than half of British exports will be from

American-owned companies, and these are highly concentrated investments. Forty percent of direct investment in Germany, France, and Britain is by three firms—American firms. George Ball has explained that the project of constructing an integrated world economy dominated by American capital—an empire, in other words—is no idealistic pipe dream, but a hardheaded prediction. It's a role, he says, into which "we have been pushed by the imperatives of our own economy," the major instrument being the multinational corporation. Through such multinational corporations, Ball suggests, it has become possible to use the world's resources with "maximum efficiency." These multinational corporations, he says, are the beneficiary of the mobilization of resources by the federal government and its worldwide operations and markets, and are backed ultimately by American military force.[48]

It is not difficult to guess who will reap the

benefits from the integrated world economy, which is the domain of operation of these American-based international economic institutions.

Well, at this stage in the discussion one has to mention the specter of communism. What is the threat of communism to this system? For a clear and cogent answer, one can turn to an extensive study of the Woodrow Wilson Foundation and National Planning Association called the *Political Economy of American Foreign Policy*, a very important book. It was compiled by a representative segment of the tiny elite that largely sets public policy for whoever is technically in office. In effect, it's as close as you can come to a manifesto of the American ruling class. Here they define the primary threat of communism as the economic transformation of the Communist powers "in ways which reduce their willingness and ability to complement the industrial economies of the West."[49] That is the primary threat of communism. Communism, in short, reduces the willingness and ability of underdeveloped countries to function in the world capitalist economy in the manner of, for example, the Philippines, which developed a colonial economy of a classic type after seventy-five years of American tutelage and domination. It's this doctrine that explains why British economist Joan Robinson describes the American crusade against communism as a crusade against development.

The Cold War ideology and the international Communist conspiracy function in an important way, as essentially a propaganda device to mobilize support at a particular historical moment for this longtime imperial enterprise. In fact, I believe that this is probably the main function of the Cold War: it serves as a useful device for the managers of American society and their counterparts in the Soviet Union to control their own populations in their own respective imperial systems. I think that the persistence of the Cold War can be, in part, explained by its utility for the managers of the two great world systems.

Well, there is one final element that has to be added to this picture, namely the ongoing militarization of American society. How does this enter in? To see how it does, one has to look back at World War II and to recall that prior to World War II, of course, we were deep in the Depression. World War II taught an important economic lesson: it taught the lesson that government-induced production in a carefully centrally controlled economy could overcome the effects of the Depression. I think that this is what Charles E. Wilson had in mind in 1944 when he proposed that we have a "permanent war economy" in the postwar world.[50] The trouble is that in a capitalist economy there are only a number of ways in which government intervention can take place. It can't be competitive with the private empires, for example, which is to say that there can't be any useful production. In fact, it has to be the production of luxury goods— not capital, not useful commodities, which would be competitive. And, unfortunately, there is only one category of luxury goods that can be produced endlessly, with rapid obsolescence, quickly wasting, and with no limit on how many of them you can use. We all know what category that is: military production.

This whole matter is described pretty well by business historian Alfred Chandler. He describes the economic lessons of World War II as follows:

> The government spent far more than the most enthusiastic New Dealer had ever proposed. Most of the output of the expenditures was destroyed or left on the battlefields of Europe and Asia. But the resulting increased demand sent the nation into a period of prosperity the like of which had never before been seen. Moreover, the supplying of huge armies and

navies fighting the most massive war of all time required a tight, centralized control of the national economy. This effort brought corporate managers to Washington to carry out one of the most complex pieces of economic planning in history. That experience lessened the ideological fears over the government's role in stabilizing the economy.[51]

This is a conservative commentator, I might point out. It may be added that the ensuing Cold War carried further the depoliticization of American society and created the kind of psychological environment in which the government is able to intervene, in part through fiscal policies, and in part through public work and public services, but very largely, of course, through defense spending.

In this way, to use Alfred Chandler's words, the government acts as "a coordinator of last resort" when "managers are unable to maintain a high level of aggregate demand."[52]

As another business historian, Joseph Monsen, writes, the enlightened corporate manager, far from fearing government intervention in the economy, "views the New Economics as a technique for increasing corporate viability."[53]

The most cynical use of these ideas is by the managers of the publicly subsidized war industries. There was a remarkable series in the *Washington Post* about a year ago by Bernard Nossiter. For example, he quoted Samuel F. Downer, vice president of LTV Aerospace, one of the big new conglomerates, who explained why the postwar world must be bolstered by military orders. "It's basic," he says.

> Its selling appeal is the defense of the home. This is one of the greatest appeals the politicians have to adjusting the system. If you're the president and you need a control factor in the economy, and you need to sell this factor, you can't sell Harlem and Watts, but you can sell self-preservation, a new environment. We are

going to increase defense budgets as long as those bastards in Russia are ahead of us. The American people understand this.[54]

Of course, "those bastards" aren't exactly ahead of us in this deadly and cynical game, but that is only a minor embarrassment to the thesis. In times of need we can always follow Dean Rusk, Hubert Humphrey, and other luminaries and appeal to the billion Chinese who are armed to the teeth and setting out on world conquest. Again, I want to emphasize the role of the Cold War in this system as a technique of domestic control, a technique for developing the climate of paranoia and psychosis in which the taxpayer will be willing to provide an enormous, endless subsidy to the technologically advanced sectors of American industry and the corporations that dominate this increasingly centralized system.

Well, of course, to stress the obvious, Russian imperialism is not an invention of American ideologists. It's real enough for the Hungarians and the Czechs, for example. What is an invention is the uses to which it is put, for example by Dean Acheson in 1950 or Walt Rostow a decade later, when they pretended that the Vietnam War was an example of Russian imperialism. Or by the Johnson administration in 1965 when it justified the Dominican intervention with reference to the Sino-Soviet military bloc. Or by the Kennedy intellectuals who, as Townsend Hoopes put it in an article in the *Washington Monthly* last month, were deluded by the "tensions of the Cold War years" and could not perceive that the triumph of national revolution in Vietnam would not be "a triumph for Moscow and Peking."[55] It was the most remarkable degree of delusion on the part of presumably literate men—or, for example, by Eugene Rostow, who, in a recent book that was very widely praised by liberal senators and academic intellectuals, outlined the series of challenges to world order in the modern era as follows: Napoleon, Kaiser Wilhelm II, Hitler, and, continuing in the post World War II world, "general strikes in Italy and France . . . the civil war in Greece, and the attacks on South Korea and South Vietnam." Russia has "put us to severe tests, like those of Korea and Vietnam," in its "efforts to spread Communism by the sword." "The forces of evil are immensely strong," and we must courageously resist them.[56]

Now, this is a very interesting series of challenges to world order: Napoleon, Kaiser Wilhelm, Hitler, general strikes in France and Italy, the civil war in Greece, and the Russian attack on South Vietnam. If one thinks it through, one can reach some pretty interesting conclusions about modern history.

Well, one can continue with this indefinitely. I mean to suggest that the Cold War is highly functional, both for the American elite and for its Soviet counterpart, who in a perfectly similar way exploit Western imperialism, which they did not invent, as they send their armies into Czechoslovakia.

In both cases, the Cold War is important in providing an ideology for empire, the government subsidized system here, and for militarized state capitalism. It's predictable, then, that the challenges to this ideology will be bitterly resisted—by force, if necessary. In many ways American society is indeed open and liberal values are preserved. However, as poor people and black people and other ethnic minorities know very well, the liberal veneer is pretty thin. Mark Twain once wrote that "it is by the goodness of God that in our country we have those three unspeakably precious things: freedom of speech, freedom of conscience, and the prudence never to practice either of them."[57] Those who lack the prudence may well pay the cost.

Roughly speaking, I think it's accurate to say that a corporate elite of managers and owners governs the economy and the political system as

well—at least in a very large measure. The so-
called people do exercise an occasional choice
among those who Marx once called "the rival
factions and adventurers of the ruling classes."[58]
And those who find this characterization too
harsh may prefer the formulations of a modern
democratic theorist like Joseph Schumpeter,
who describes modern political democracy,
favorably, as the system in which "the deciding
of issues by the electorate [is] secondary to the
election of the men who are to do the deciding."
The political party, he says, quite accurately, "is
a group whose members propose to act in con-
cert in competitive struggle for political power.
If that were not so, it would be impossible for different parties to adopt exactly or almost exactly
the same program."[59] Those are the advantages
of the political democracy, as Schumpeter sees it.

This is a program that both parties adopt
more or less exactly. The individuals who com-
pete for power express a narrow conservative

ideology, basically the interests of one or another sector of the corporate elite, with some modifications. Now, this is obviously no conspiracy. I think it is simply implicit in the system of corporate capitalism. These people and the institutions they represent are in effect in power, and their interests are the "national interest." It is this interest that is served, primarily and overwhelmingly, by the overseas empire and the growing system of military state capitalism at home. If we were to withdraw the consent of the governed, as I think we should, we are withdrawing our consent to have these men—and the interests they represent—govern and manage American society and impose their concept of world order and their criteria for legitimate political and economic development on much of the world. Although an immense effort of propaganda and mystification is carried on to conceal these facts, nonetheless facts they remain.

We have today the technical and material resources to meet man's animal needs. We have not developed the cultural and moral resources—or the democratic forms of social organization—that make possible the humane and rational use of our material wealth and power. Conceivably, the classical liberal ideals as expressed and developed in their libertarian socialist form are achievable. But if so, only by a popular revolutionary movement, rooted in a wide strata of the population and committed to the elimination of repressive and authoritarian institutions, state and private. To create such a movement is a challenge we face and must meet if there is to be an escape from contemporary barbarism.

Notes

1   Wilhelm von Humboldt, *Limits of State Action*, J. W. Burrow, ed.
    (London: Cambridge University Press, 1969), chap. 7, p. 68.
2   Von Humboldt, *Limits of State Action,* chap. 8, p. 76.
3   Von Humboldt, *Limits of State Action,* chap. 7, p. 62 and chap.
    3, p. 19.
4   Von Humboldt, *Limits of State Action,* chap. 3, p. 19.
5   Von Humboldt, *Limits of State Action,* chap. 3, p. 22.
6   Von Humboldt, "Ideas on Constitutional Statehood, Incited
    by the New French Constitution" (from a Letter to a Friend,
    August 1791), cited in Marianne Cowan, ed., *Humanist
    Without Portfolio: An Anthology* (Detroit: Wayne State
    University Press, 1964).
7   Cited in Shlomo Avineri, *The Social and Political Thought of
    Karl Marx* (London: Cambridge University Press, 1968),
    p. 142, referring to comments in *The Holy Family.* See Robert
    C. Tucker, ed., *The Marx–Engels Reader,* 2nd ed. (New York:
    W. W. Norton, 1972), pp. 133–35.

8   Karl Marx, *Critique of the Gotha Program,* part I, sec. 3. In
    Tucker, ed., *The Marx–Engels Reader,* p. 388.

9   Karl Marx, *Capital,* part 5, chap 25, sec. 4. In Tucker, ed. *The
    Marx–Engels Reader,* p. 310.

10 Rudolf Rocker, *Anarcho-Syndicalism: Theory and Practice*
    (Oakland: AK Press, 2004), p. 10.

11 Karl Polanyi, *The Great Transformation: The Political and
    Economic Origins of Our Time* (Boston: Beacon Press, 1957),
    p. 3.

12 Polanyi, *The Great Transformation,* p. 176.

13 Simon Linguet, *Théorie des lois civiles* (London, 1767), pp.
    274, 464, 466, 470–71, cited in Karl Marx, *Theories of Surplus
    Value* [Volume IV of *Capital*], Part I (1863), S. Ryazanskaya,
    ed., Emile Burns, trans. (Moscow: Progress Publishers, 1963),
    chap. 7, pp. 346, 348, 349.

14 Cited in Martin Buber, *Paths in Utopia* (Boston: Beacon Press,
    1958), p. 19.

15 Von Humboldt, *The Limits of State Action,* chap. 16, p. 137.

16 Jean-Jacques Rousseau, *First and Second Discourses,* R. D.
    Masters, ed. (New York: St. Martin's Press, 1964), p. 179.

17 Von Humboldt, *Limits of State Action,* chap. 11, pp. 99–100.

18 Octave Mirbeau, quoted in James Joll, *The Anarchists* (Boston:
    Little, Brown, 1965), pp. 145–46.

19 Quoted in Daniel Guérin, *Anarchism: From Theory to Practice,*
    Mary Klopper, trans. (New York: Monthly Review, 1970), p. 12.

20 Pierre-Joseph Proudhon, *What Is Property?* Benjamin R. Tucker,
    trans. (New York: Howard Fertig, Inc., 1966), chap. 1, p. 12.

21 Anton Pannekoek, "Theses On The Fight Of The Working
    Class   Against   Capitalism"   (1947).   Online   at:
    http://www.marxists.org/archive/pannekoe/1947/theses-
    fight.htm. Transcribed from *Southern Advocate for Workers
    Councils,* Melbourne, Australia, no. 33, May 1947.

22 See V. I. Lenin, *Left-Wing Communism: An Infantile Disorder* (Moscow: Progress Publishers, 1964).

23 William Paul, *The State: Its Origins and Function* (Glasgow: Socialist Labour Press, 1918), pp. 197–98.

24 *Informations Correspondance Ouvrière.*

25 A later version of this paper is available online: Walter Kendall, "State Ownership, Workers' Control and Socialism," paper presented at the First International Sociological Conference on Participation and Self-Management, Dubrovnik, December 13–17, 1972 (http://www.whatnextjournal.co.uk/Pages/Newint/Kendall2.html).

26 Letter from Engels to Philipp Van Patten, April 18, 1883. Available online at: http://www.marxists.org/archive/marx/works/1883/letters/83_04_18.htm.

27 The preface to the German edition of 1872. In Tucker, ed., *The Marx–Engels Reader,* pp. 469–70.

28 Quoted in Guérin, *Anarchism,* p. 25.

29 Quoted in Guérin, *Anarchism,* pp. 25–26.

30 Fernand Pelloutier, "Anarchism and the Workers' Unions," in Daniel Guérin, ed., *No Gods, No Masters,* 2 vols. (Oakland: AK Press, 1998), vol. 2, p. 55.

31 Buber, *Paths in Utopia,* p. 127.

32 V. I. Lenin, *Sochineniya* (*Works*), 5th ed. (Moscow: Institute of Marxism-Leninism, 1958–65), vol. 44, pp. 9 and 418. Quoted in Moshe Lewin, *Lenin's Last Struggle,* A. M. Sheridan Smith, trans. (New York: Pantheon, 1968), p. 4.

33 Rousseau, *First and Second Discourses,* p. 164.

34 Rousseau, *First and Second Discourses,* p. 165.

35 Immanuel Kant, *Religion within the Limits of Reason Alone,* 1793, Book 4, Part 2, Section 3.

36 Wilhelm von Humboldt, *Limits of State Action,* chap. 16, p. 143.

37 Von Humboldt, *Limits of State Action,* chap. 3, p. 18.

NOAM CHOMSKY

38 Rosa Luxemburg, "Organizational Questions of the Russian
   Social Democracy ['Leninism or Marxism?']" (1904), Part II.
   Available online at: http://www.marxists.org/archive/luxem-
   burg/1904/questions-rsd/index.htm.

39 Carl Kaysen, "The Social Significance of the Modern
   Corporation," *American Economic Review*, May 1957,
   pp. 313–14.

40 See Ralph Miliband, *The State in Capitalist Society* (London:
   Weidenfield & Nicolson, 1969).

41 Richard J. Barnet, *The Economy of Death* (New York:
   Atheneum, 1969), p. 97.

42 House Report 1406, 87th Cong., 2nd sess., 1962, p. 7.

43 Arthur H. Vandenberg, Jr., *The Private Papers of Senator
   Vandenberg* (Boston: Houghton-Mifflin, 1952), p. 504.

44 Robert McNamara, *The Essence of Security* (New York: Harper
   & Row, 1968), pp. 109–10.

45 McNamara, *The Essence of Security*, p. 110.

46 *Economic Concentration,* Hearings Before the Subcommittee on
   Antitrust and Monopoly of the Committee on the Judiciary,
   U.S. Senate, 91st Congress, 1st Session (1969), Part 8A.

47 Leo Model, "The Politics of Private Foreign Investment,"
   Foreign Affairs, June 1967, p. 641.

48 George W. Ball, *The Discipline of Power: Essentials of a Modern
   World Structure* (Boston: Atlantic Monthly Press, 1968).

49 W. Y. Elliot, ed., *The Political Economy of American Foreign
   Policy* (New York: Henry Holt and Co., 1955), p. 42.

50 Quoted in Barnet, *The Economy of Death,* p. 116.

51 Alfred D. Chandler, Jr., "The Role of Business in the United
   States: A Historical Survey," *Daedalus,* winter 1969, p. 36.

52 Chandler, Jr., "The Role of Business in the United States," p. 36.

53 Joseph Monsen, "The American Business View," *Daedalus,*
   winter 1969, p. 162.

GOVERNMENT IN THE FUTURE

GOVERNMENT IN THE FUTURE

54 Bernard Nossiter, "Arms Firms See Postwar Spurt," *Washington Post*, December 8, 1968, pp. A1, A18.
55 Townsend Hoopes, "The Nuremberg Suggestion," *Washington Monthly*, January 1970, p. 20.
56 Eugene Rostow, *Law, Power and the Pursuit of Power* (Lincoln: University of Nebraska Press, 1968), pp. 13, 17, 47.
57 "Pudd'nhead Wilson's New Calendar," from *Following the Equator*, in Tom Quirk, ed., *Tales, Speeches, Essays, and Sketches* (New York: Penguin, 1994), p. 201.
58 "The Civil War in France," in Tucker, ed., *The Marx–Engels Reader*, p. 630.
59 Joseph Schumpeter, *Capitalism, Socialism, and Democracy* (New York: Harper & Row, 1950), pp. 269, 283.

Special thanks to Krishna Pagadala for transcription,
to Pablo Stafforini for revision and references, and
to Crystal Yakacki for excellent research.